The UnKept Heart

Tamara D. Pope

DEDICATION

This book is dedicated to those who suffer from
broken hearts, wounded hearts, and heavy hearts.
I pray through the pages of this book
that the Father by way of His Spirit exposes the true
source of your wounding.

TABLE OF CONTENTS

ACKNOWLEDGMENTS

There are so many who have contributed to this work. I want to pause and thank each of you. All that you've done is appreciated.

To my Husband, David, who continually supports my dreams and patiently travels with me emotionally, mentally, and physically as I put on paper that which brews inside of me, I love you forever.

To my Children, Dante', Aurielle, and Alyse, who believe in and encourage me with each new venture, I do this for you. Never stop dreaming. Never stop pursuing. Never stop believing. I love you forever.

To my Parents, Wilson and Gladys Daniels, for your continual example of sacrificial love and the power of Faith, your labor is not in vain. I love you forever.

To my Brother, Tony, never stop pushing, never stop trying, never stop believing. I love you forever.

To my Ministry Partners & Editorial Team, Annie, Chandra, Marsha, Sally, Takisha, and Violet, thank you for all that you do. I love you forever.

To the wonderful group of women who walk with me daily through our Transformation Sessions, thank you for serving as the proving ground for our ministry. I love you forever.

Introduction

"Say something!" **"What do you want me to say?"**
"Tell them to stop! Let them know that this isn't okay!"
**"If I tell them, they might become angry and no longer
desire to deal with me."** *"This makes no sense to me.
Why would you allow this to happen repeatedly? They
keep doing the same things over and over again. Say
something! Why are we even here? What? Where did
you go? Great!!!!! With no warning, you just disappear!
I can't believe it! You just left me here. You left me all
alone. This is not good for me. When I need you the
most, you abandon me. Now what am I supposed to do?
It's so dark and unfriendly in here. Nothing is clear. I
don't recognize anyone. Where am I? What am I doing
here? We came together, but now I can't find you.
Everyone is operating as if this is the norm, but nothing
about this is normal. At least, not my norm. Where did
you go? Please say something to me. Your silence has
me in agony. I don't like how this feels. My heart is
racing. No it's hurting. Now it's racing. No it's hurting.
This is not funny! If this is supposed to be a joke, it's a
cruel joke. I don't find it funny. I'm not laughing.*

*They've isolated me and now they are picking at me. Hey! Stop! That hurts! I see you now. Why aren't you helping me? Stop! What is wrong with them? Why are they picking at me again? You're hurting me!!!!! Why do they keep digging in the same space! Stop! It's already tender and hurting from your initial assaults. What is their problem? I'm begging you to help me. You're just sitting there looking, not engaging. I can't do this alone! Help me! I don't like this place. Did you know they were going to hurt me when you left me? I pray you didn't intentionally leave me here for them to hurt me. Can't you feel what's going on? Were you aware they were going to do this to me? They are mistreating me. No one is helping me. I don't know what to think. I don't know what to believe. It doesn't make sense that you would just leave. If you love me, why would you leave me? How could you just abandon me? Stop!" "**They can't hear you**." "Finally, you respond to me. I know I'm crying out internally. I'm afraid if I say anything externally they will abandon me, and I'd prefer they mistreat me rather than abandon me.*

~ The Battle Within ~ Me

This battle within me is such a familiar place. I've been here before. This is not a new space. How did I end up here again? I was on the upswing and God was doing a new thing. Enlarging me by leaps and bounds. Even granting me access to new ground. I don't understand what happened here. As I reminisce on this place, familiarity slaps me in the face. I've been here before. Ten years ago I made the declaration, *"It's My Time to Deal With It! I'm Overcoming Strongholds."* Yes, that was my coming out of the closet year. My year of exposure, I was no longer hiding. I began my journey of uncovering what was at operation within me in my quest to free my family. I look at this place ten years later and I see that I exposed, but I'm not sure if I actually expelled the enemy. When you expose but don't expel, the place grows darker, and runs deeper.

I'm not giving up my fight. My legacy is not quitter, but overcomer and this is not just for me, but for my legacy. This one is for my family!

Tamara D. Pope, The UnKept Heart

❦ 1 ❧

WHAT HAPPENED TO ME?

My mind was racing and tears were falling from my eyes so rapidly I couldn't focus. I needed to pull over to regain my composer before continuing my drive home. *"Parking lot",* I thought. *"The first parking lot I see will work for me",* I said internally.

Devastated does not adequately describe my state at that moment. While driving and crying, I was trying to understand, *"What had just happened to me? Why does this keep happening to me?"* I had been deeply wounded and needed to regroup so that I could make it home. The tears wouldn't stop, streaks of mascara were running down my face, and everything was becoming blurry. *"Home, I just want to get home"*, I said internally.

Barely able to see in front of me, I turned into the first parking lot I approached and stopped fighting the flow of tears that were desperately trying to exit my eyes. That parking lot served as my purging place. It wasn't the place I would have chosen, but I had lost control so it would have to do. My body was letting go of that which I had internalized. It was releasing things I pretended didn't bother me, and that I was trying to hide. My body had been waiting for a moment to let go, to get it out, to release. The tears that just wouldn't stop were my body's way of cleansing, purging, and releasing.

While gasping for air between each outburst of tears, I called my husband. My heart yearned for the safety and assurance of his embrace. He's my safe place. If anyone could fix this, surely he could. There's nothing he wouldn't do for me. My mind drifted back to a breakdown I'd experienced some years prior to this one during which I reached out to my husband. I was hurting, my heart was broken, and I was trying to deal with issues that had tormented me for years.

Just as with my current dilemma, I was driving trying to continue with my normal activity as though what I was experiencing had not broken me in some way. How did I know that something in me had broken? Something in me had disconnected. Broken. Something was not right inside of me. Broken. I couldn't muster up a smile and I smile naturally. Broken. Before speaking or taking action I consider and think it through and on that day I couldn't even think rationally. Broken. Optimistic, hopeful is how most would describe me, but my hope had been hindered and I had no expectation of anything good.

Broken was my condition on that day, and my husband's response to my reach was, *"Meet me at home."* When I arrived home, he embraced me, reassured me of his love for me, and that he was there and wasn't going anywhere. He let me know he wouldn't abandon me, and no matter how unpleasant it was that he would not run out on me. In that moment, I felt the Father loving me through my husband. That day, through my husband the Father won my heart again.

In that moment on that day in the parking lot, I needed that assurance again. *"Hello"*, my husband answered. It was a welcome interruption to my moment of reminiscing. There was this tone in his voice that always assures me that everything is going to be alright. Just hearing his voice on the other end of the phone brought calm to my state of hysteria. Although the tears continued to rush down my face as I spoke with him, it was reassuring to know that I was not alone. He listened attentively surrendering his ears to my ranting. Before hanging up he asked, *"Where are you?"* I replied, *"In the Office Depot parking lot."* He responded, *"I'll meet you at home."* Just what I needed to hear! Allowing myself the time needed to pull it together so that I could drive home, I sat in that parking lot a little while longer. While sitting there, I couldn't help but wonder, *"What went wrong?"* *"Where did I go wrong?"* *This should not be happening to me.*

When I began writing this book, my first thought was to use a fictitious name. This would (I thought) allow me the freedom to be completely transparent. You know what I mean. It was an opportunity to disclose all. Included would be details regarding the wounds I had suffered, the scars that remained, and how I had been mishandled, mistreated. *"What if I also give those involved, the individuals who wounded me, fictitious names?"* I pondered. We would be covered, and it would add an element of mystery leaving the readers wondering, *"Who is this woman?"* *"Who are these people?"* Simultaneously, the fictitious name would cover me. You would get to know my offenders and me without knowing it was us. Without those who wounded me knowing, I could talk about it. Air my dirty laundry, and receive sympathy maybe some empathy. It would help me. Without letting them know they've wounded me, or discussing with them how it's affected me, I could release it. Get it off of my chest. You see, I figured the fictitious name would provide a shield for me. It would block me. Any comments made or judgments shared would be towards the character created not towards me.

Yes, I had thought it out. It sounded like a plan, but just as quickly as I entertained the thought of using fictitious names, I dismissed the notion. *"What was I doing? What was I considering?"* That would be reverting for me. Instead of moving forward, I would be going backward. As I considered returning to a lifestyle of hiding, I was quickly convicted. Hiding has not been the nature of my journey. I was in the light. My journey was one of exposure, shedding light on the dark areas in my life. Choosing to hide would set me back even further. It would send me deeper into the darkness than I was when I initially came out. I CANNOT GO BACK! BACK IS NOT AN OPTION FOR ME! WHAT WAS BACK THERE ALMOST KILLED ME!

I immediately interrupted this train of thought and reminded myself, *"You are a Woman of Word (WOW).* Allow me to define a "WOW!" for our purposes. A "WOW!" is a Woman who studies the Word of God. 2 Timothy 2:15 NLT says, *"Work hard so you can present yourself to God and receive his approval. Be a good worker, one who does not need to be ashamed and who*

correctly explains the word of truth." A "WOW!"
devotes time to study. The focus of her study is the
Word of God. Regularly reading and researching for
understanding is a priority for A "WOW!" She realizes
to accurately apply and share The Word of God that she
must know it and understand it. She invests time in study
and makes it a priority daily. A "WOW!" also knows the
Word of God. Psalm 119:11 NLT says, *"I have hidden
your word in my heart, that I might not sin against you."*
She understands that her study must become more than
gathering information to acquire knowledge, but it must
become a part of her. Meditating on and internalizing the
Word is critical. She realizes what she allows to reside
within shapes her thinking and living. It also affects how
she processes the various experiences she will encounter.
Finally, A "WOW!" lives this way because she loves the
Lord. John 14:23 NLT says, *Jesus replied, "All who
love me will do what I say. My Father will love them, and
we will come and make our home with each of them."*
She lives out her love for the Father through obedience to
Him. Her relationship with Him is the motivation for
what she does or doesn't give herself over to. The

demonstration of her love for Him is witnessed in how she loves, lives, gives, and forgives.

Yep! I am a "WOW!" But what a minute, with all of this Word in me, what happened to me? What's going on inside of me? How did I end up in this parking lot broken again? There I was considering using fictitious names, trying to hide again; but, I thought I no longer engaged in those games. I had been delivered, rescued from living a life full of shame.

Sitting in that lot distraught over what someone had done to me, I realized that moment was not about them but all about me. What had just transpired didn't even matter. The Father wanted to use that situation to show me how I had neglected me. That day's occurrence was not an isolated event, but there was a pattern that had been established. A habit had developed. Negligence wasn't foreign to me, but until that day I didn't realize what it had done to me.

ᏣᏅ2ᏭᎤ

EXPOSED BUT NOT EXPELLED

There I was sitting in that parking lot trying to catch my breath so that I could regroup, and go home; but, each attempt was met with another thought or reminder. Each thought seemed to be awakening dormant areas within me that I thought I had handled and were healed; but, this current dilemma was producing pain that proved they hadn't been handled, and that I wasn't healed. It was as if old wounds within me were being revived in the form of offense.

As the pain associated with each offense began to consume me, it quickly turned into anger. Memories, reminders, and snippets of these past experiences were bombarding my mind. It was as if someone had turned on an old movie inside of me. The opening scene was a compilation of occurrences in which I'd given my all, the very best of what I had to offer, and instead of being embraced I was used up and replaced.

As these snippets of my life continued to play, feelings of being mishandled were resurrected within me. Watching these scenes replay left me feeling what I had to offer in each circumstance wasn't good enough. With each snippet of this old movie that ran through my mind, these feelings grew stronger and traveled even deeper. Anger then turned to despair and tears began to fall again as feelings of inadequacy and that I was not enough overwhelmed me.

These old scenes rekindled old feelings that ran through me like a power surge. I could hear myself thinking, *"You're replaceable, disposable, and unnecessary. They just tolerate you until they can find the one they really want. You are just a filler, a temp, a substitute. You always have been and always will be. Their intention never is to keep you. You're not the real deal. There's really nothing special about you. See, they've moved on because you're not worth the investment. You're not worth the time. You're broken and no one wants to spend time with broken people. Although you are giving everything you have in the midst of being broken, no one has the desire, energy, or time to walk with you while the Father works on you. Don't you get it yet? Even when you have something to offer, it's not you that they desire it's what you have or do. When you can no longer do, they no longer want you. You have no value without what you do. To them, you're useless. They have no desire to know you. No, they don't want a relationship with you. There is nothing special about you. They don't want you. You're broken."*

Oh no! It was back! That old fear had been realized again. The fear of being rejected, not being accepted had been resurrected, and its presence was stronger. In pain and now angry again, I continued this conversation with myself. I asked, *"Why Me? Why do people always*

mistreat and take advantage of me? What is it about me?
If the same thing keeps happening over and over again is
it really everyone else or is it me? When they mistreat
me, why don't I say anything? Why do I allow them to do
this repeatedly? Why don't I stand up for myself? I'm a
WOW! With all of this Word in me, shouldn't I recognize
when this is happening to me? By now, shouldn't I
recognize people's intentions toward me? And even
when I recognize it, why don't I respond accordingly?

Right in the midst of the scenes playing over and over in
my head of wrongs committed against me by others,
previews of my involvement began popping up. It was
painful to see, but I needed to see. The flow of tears
began to pick up as I saw scenes of things I did to
encourage and approve their actions. Other scenarios
were playing where I did nothing to prevent what was
going on. It was difficult to watch, and even more
difficult to admit that one of the culprits was me.
Everything wasn't the fault of others. Please don't
misunderstand my train of thought. I'm not justifying the
wrongs committed against me by others, but I needed to

take an honest look at how I ended up in this place. How did I end up in this place again? That's right. This was not the first time I had been broken, but this time I wanted to know, I needed to know why I seemed to experience this repeatedly and oftentimes with the same people.

"Come on Tam, get it together! You need to go home!" I told myself still sitting in the parking lot attempting to calm down enough to drive home. *"Ten Years!"* I yelled. *"It's been ten years!"* The old movie running in my head had changed scenes. It was now playing out the beginning of my journey ten years ago to address what was broken in me. Everything began with me.

I had a desire to help others walk in victory, but first it needed to happen for me. That's where it started, that's where it all began, but somewhere in the process I stopped working on me and began focusing on fixing others. My broken state, sitting in that parking lot, brought everything to an abrupt stop. Right in the middle of preparing to help others move through their season of brokenness to a place of comfort, confrontation, and healing, everything for me came to a halt. While preparing to help them through their crisis, I was facing my own personal crisis. This meltdown caused me to question everything. Not only was I questioning everything, I began doubting everything. It stopped me dead in my tracks. It was time to take a look at what was happening to me. I needed the Father to fix it. I needed Him to fix me.

As I watched this scene that had occurred over ten years ago playing out in my mind, I began reliving that life-changing moment in time. This scene began with me on my knees in my bathroom praying. During that afternoon of prayer, I was crying out to the Lord for my family. While seeking the Father regarding them, He began speaking to me about me. As I pressed in regarding my family, the Lord gave me instructions for me regarding me.

In that bathroom, the Father began dealing with me regarding what was broken in me. He showed me where

I lacked integrity. Yep! Dishonesty, a lying spirit was ruling from within me. I knew it was there, but I needed help correcting it, getting rid of it, stopping it. I was broken.

I would lie to convince others that what wasn't really was, and to alter reality. The intent was to deceive and manipulate people into liking and accepting me. No matter what the reason it was opposed to Truth which makes sense because God is Truth, *"Jesus told him, "I am the way, the truth, and the life. No one can come to the Father except through me."* John 14:6 NLT. The devil is the Father of lies. *"For you are the children of your father the devil and you love to do the evil things he does. He was a murderer from the beginning. He has always hated the truth, because there is no truth in him. When he lies, it is consistent with his character; for he is a liar and the father of lies."* John 8:44 NLT. Daily, the battle in me between the Spirit of God, The Truth, and the devil, the liar, for control of me was intensifying. *"The sinful nature wants to do evil, which is just the opposite of what the Spirit wants. And the Spirit gives us desires that are the opposite of what the sinful nature desires. These two forces are constantly fighting each other, so you are not free to carry out your good intentions."* Galatians 5:17 NLT. The Father, The Truth was exposing this lying spirit at operation inside of me. This deceiving and manipulating spirit had been working in many forms through me. The Father wanted to help me, free me, and prepare me, so that He could use me as a testimony to walk with others in their quest for liberty. Before I could walk with them, I had to walk with Him. This was my coming out party.

Sitting in my car thinking about that season in my life caused conviction to stir, and the tears that I thought were coming to an end began to flow again. I found comfort as I remembered that, *"But if we confess our sins to him, he is faithful and just to forgive us our sins and to cleanse us from all wickedness."* 1 John 1:9 NLT.

Watching this portion of the snippets of my journey was especially challenging for me emotionally. This particular scene began with the Father challenging me to confess wrongs I had committed. Some of these moments were in private and others were public. There were some individuals I was to contact personally and to others, the confessions were made publicly.

Whew! I remember feeling shame, embarrassment, guilt, uncovered, discovered, exposed, and vulnerable initially; and, then I noticed something happening. The more I confessed, the more comfortable I became with confessing publically. Watching the snippets replay in my mind I noticed my transitioning from shame to what was perceived as fame. I was relieved and living life openly. As a matter of fact, confession created a platform for me to share my story. Sharing my story actually helped and allowed me the opportunity to release those things that I had been hiding. Lying was a form of hiding for me. It allowed me to create my own reality and shape what people thought about me.

All I wanted was to be accepted. Not hiding or trying to cover felt so good! My confessions weren't focused on others, but where I had messed up and caused misery.

Coming clean about those hidden things was refreshing. I allowed the light to shine on the darkness inside of me.

As I continued watching the old movie, I noticed something disturbing. Confessing I was doing regularly, but I never moved on to addressing the lack of integrity – the lying spirit in me. Although I talked about it regularly, I realized this spirit had been exposed, but never expelled. It was still at operation within me! *"JESUS!"* I yelled as I made this discovery.

Confessing is being honest about your condition, but addressing is doing something about your condition. Confessing was where I began, but I still had a long way to go. Although I was being brutally honest about what was transpiring in my life, I hadn't done anything to address it. Year after year I was telling the story, but continuing to do the same things. The only thing that had changed was that I was talking about it. I was still broken. The problem still existed. I still lacked integrity and a lying spirit was still controlling me, but I was talking.

This spirit continued to grow and infect my life and the lives of others, but I was talking. Not only had it survived, but it had also begun to thrive. You see sharing the story gave it notoriety, a platform. People seemed to enjoy hearing me talk about how broken, and messed up I was. It entertained and captivated audiences as I openly shared my struggle, my brokenness. This gained exposure moved me into new territory.

Although I was confessing, telling the truth about me, I was not applying the truth to my situation. I knew the Word, the Truth, but in order to be set free, I needed to apply the Word, the Truth. Ringing in my ear I could hear, *"If you are hearing the Word and not applying the Word, then you are walking in self deception. But don't just listen to God's word. You must do what it says. Otherwise, you are only fooling yourselves."* James 1:22 NLT. That was me. I had exposed - confessed what was going on in me, but I hadn't expelled – addressed it. Wow!

My attitude was here I am wounded, bruised, imperfect,

broken, and I am accepted. Just the way I am I'm accepted. If I never change I am accepted. I deceived myself into believing that confession was completion. The Father desired that I not only confess I lacked integrity and was a liar; but, that I also stop doing it! Revelation! Ten years ago the work was started in me; but, it wasn't completed. I considered it a closed case when in reality it was still open and incomplete! Walking in self-deception made it difficult to determine when others were being truthful or deceiving me.

You see, I wanted to believe and be accepted so badly that I would make what others said my truth, but making it my truth did not mean it was the truth. I altered my reality. It was difficult to determine what was real and what was fantasy. Although their actions were demonstrating the opposite of what I desired, I still wanted to believe that their motives were pure. So I began making excuses for their behavior and convincing myself that it wasn't what I was seeing; and, that I was misinterpreting what was happening. Even though the truth was right there in front of me, I would convince myself that it really wasn't what I was seeing. You see, if it were what I was seeing, that would make them deceitful, manipulative, and that just couldn't be. I had spent so much time avoiding addressing the lack of integrity; yes that lying spirit at operation within me, that I was afraid. This fear stripped me of the power to address deception and manipulation in me and with those who mishandled me. *"You say I am empowered by Satan. But if Satan is divided and fighting against himself, how can his kingdom survive?"* Luke 11:18 NLT. That which I was refused to address kept me shackled to the same old mess.

Over ten years ago, I exposed but never expelled that which was going on inside of me. It didn't go away, but it grew and gained more territory.

∞3∞

SLACK BROUGHT ME BACK

It's difficult to discern a thing when you're in a thing and have not been delivered from that thing. When it has its grips on you, it's challenging to determine what reality is and what's not true.

Sitting in my car in that parking lot, I realized I was so consumed with my false reality that the world I created became true to me. This false reality had shaped everything for me. I had created this place in which I thought I was controlling my space. Whew! You don't realize how lost you are until the truth you are ready to see, and sitting in that parking lot I was ready.

"I'm tired of people getting over on me and being afraid they won't accept me. Living life afraid to let people know they hurt me because they might become angry with me. I'm sick of being afraid of how they'll view me and what they might tell others about me. Hiding how I feel because they might end the relationship with me. Now I'm overthinking every move. Being so paralyzed with fear that I don't do anything because I'm afraid I'll do the wrong thing. So I constantly shy away from taking risks preferring to play it safe. Well, at least I know here what to expect even if I'm just pretending. I'm not alone. I'm accepted. Even if it's a false sense of who I am, it's accepted. So, I'll take this over being alone, rejected, disrespected, unappreciated, misunderstood, and...wait a minute! No! I'm tired of living this way! I'm tired, I'm tired, I AM TIRED!!!!!" I yelled while beating my steering wheel in an effort to release some of my frustration and pain.

"Wait!!!!! Am I back here? When did this happen? How did this happen?" I asked bewildered as I tried to pull it together and regain my composure. At that

34

moment I realized I was right back where I had started ten years ago. The only thing that had changed was my situation. Different situation, same struggle, same manifestation, and the root had grown deeper. This was a bit much for me because I thought … I had convinced myself that I was free.

This thing at operation within me, insecurity, fear of rejection and not being accepted, I was sure I had beaten and that it did not control me. It couldn't. Could it? Just then thoughts and snippets from the last ten years of my life began to race through my mind like a movie again. The scenes that were playing prompted me to look at me. It was time to examine me. Enough was enough and I needed to know why this was repeatedly happening to me. Answers… I needed answers. *"Please show me why this happens continually."* I pleaded desperately. *"What happened to me? What's going on inside of me? Why won't this thing let me be?" "Why does it keep resurfacing in me?"* I asked during this self-interrogation.

I had put in the work I thought necessary to overcome,

and defeat the demons that had me shackled in this place. Studying and praying, fasting and praying, crying and praying, denying and praying, separating myself and praying. My goal was to clean house. That's what I had set out to do. Getting rid of pretense, camouflage, and masking was not an easy chore. Ten years ago I started the journey of transparency. I remember telling my mother, *"Mom, it's like I'm learning how to live!"* I asked The Father to show me, reveal the truth to me in every area of my life. I had no desire to walk in ignorance. If I didn't know the truth, if I couldn't truly see who I was dealing with, then I would remain prime target for deception and manipulation. I was no longer interested in living that way. So I needed to see. I wanted to see. *"Remember!"* I said internally, *"I'm a WOW!"* and the Word says, " *Stay alert! Watch out for your great enemy, the devil. He prowls around like a roaring lion, looking for someone to devour."* 1 Peter 5:7 NLT. I needed to see, I wanted to see who was strategically working against me. With this knowledge, I would be more intentional. It was time to be open to what the Spirit had to say. *"When the Spirit of truth comes, he will guide you into all truth. He will not speak on his own but will tell you what he has heard. He will tell you about the future."* John 16:13 NLT. I needed revelation.

The first place revelation needed to hit was within me. I needed to know the role I was playing in what was repeatedly happening to me. Although others were involved, I was not without blame. There was something that I was or wasn't doing that kept bringing me back to this place of pain.

As painful as it might be, it was time for me to truly take a look at what was wrong with me. Yes, it was time to face it. I had already declared victory through Christ Jesus, and that I had overcome through the shed blood of the lamb. So, why was I still bound with fear? Why were the remnants of insecurity still there? Why wasn't my life bearing the fruit of what I said, but looked like what remained instead?

This struggle, this space was causing me to grow weary. I began to think, *"God isn't answering",* and I began to question, *"Why isn't the Word working?"* Not only was it affecting me, but it began to breed doubt in those who were taking their cue for living from my life. As they observed expectations which had been spoken remaining yet unmet, disappointment magnified and instead of being drawn to Christ, they rejected Him. They began a search for another way, another truth because the truth I was following didn't appear to be reliable. I should have heeded the warning to, *"Look after each other so that none of you fails to receive the grace of God. Watch out that no poisonous root of bitterness grows up to trouble you, corrupting many."* Hebrews 12:15 NLT.

"I see, I see, I see! Yes, Holy Spirit! Please continue to show me!" I cried out as He began to reveal to me the role I played in my current dilemma. It was becoming clearer to me. The Platform had taken over in me. Helping others became more important than taking care of me. I was living dangerously and had stopped paying attention to me. My well being was no longer priority.

The confession platform had consumed me. Each open

door convinced me that I had reached another plateau. I had stopped focusing on addressing the issue that existed within me. My actions demonstrated that I thought it was no longer necessary. Helping others did not necessitate first taking care of me. The solution to their dilemma was to confess like me because it was liberating.

So many appeared to be helped or were they really? I even felt like I was finally free. Yes, I thought I had been liberated from the need to hide to camouflage, and to pretend like what was going on inside of me didn't exist. There was no longer the need to live a double life. One image on the outside while inside someone completely different was living. It was difficult masking and managing what face would fit in which situation. Keeping up with the various versions of me that would surface in various situations was draining!

I began living as if I had arrived. The necessity to study and pray with the intensity that began my journey left me. In my beginnings, it was a priority and now it was relegated to whenever there was time. Besides, I had this. I could handle it. I knew the way. I felt it no longer took all of that every day. The tears that were falling again were creating puddles in my hands as I covered my eyes. Shaking my head I had to admit what was being revealed. I had begun to slack and pull back from that which led me to confession. The road to confession was a great beginning, but once I reached confession I treated it as the ending. As if the process were complete, my priority of the Father first dwindled. I didn't realize the enemy was using this as an opportunity to slowly lure me away from the path of liberty.

My heart was no longer pure. The decisions I was making were no longer guided by the Spirit. Pride had crept in and was in control leaving me vulnerable to whatever would transpire next. Living in my own wisdom I was ill-equipped to recognize deceit and I was back in the enemies net. It was my doing. My slack brought it back.

That day sitting in my car in the Office Depot parking lot, I was faced with what was happening in me. It was necessary. It was revelatory. Yes, I needed revelation. Still no resolution, but I was beginning to see what was happening to me. That which was operating in me was being revealed to me. I started the process over ten years ago, but slack had brought me back to where I had begun.

ೞ34ೲ

THE HEART ATTACK

Honesty. Okay, it was clear. I needed to be honest. *"Face it! It's not just them. It's also me. I opened the door."* I had to admit as the tears flowing from my eyes were beginning to dry.

"But this still should not be happening to me!" I said repeatedly. *"I trusted them. I trusted them with me, and that they wouldn't mistreat me. How could they do this with no regard for me? Did they even consider me? I thought they wanted the best for me, and that they approached me selflessly. I really believed they cared for me as I cared for them. That they thought of me as I*

thought of them. In my mind I thought we were growing in relationship, and that they wanted me near. I thought they valued me as much as I valued them. Our conversations suggested to me that we were on the same page. For a while, it appeared we would benefit mutually so I welcomed them into my space. Inside of me, they held a special place. What happened? Where did things turn?

"Snap out of it! I sternly said shaking my head. *" This is not a fairy tale. This is reality. Stop deceiving yourself. You have a real enemy. He wants to make your life a living hell. "* I yelled. This was real. Sitting in that parking lot staring into space, I was now facing the damage that had been done in me because of me. I was not claiming victim status because I could have avoided my current dilemma. If only I had taken better care of me. I'm beginning to see. The Spirit was showing me clearly and reminded me, *"Guard your heart above all else, for it determines the course of your life. "* Proverbs 4:23 NLT. My mistake was not looking out for me. Protecting me was my responsibility. Here I was

expecting others to see me, protect me, be gentle with me, and treat me tenderly. I was attempting to shift the responsibility. The problem wasn't those who hurt me. It was me. I was to be the guardian of my heart. By not making it my priority, I neglected me. I did it. It was me. I was assisting the enemy with destroying me by expecting others to do for me what I should have been doing for myself.

Sitting in that parking lot I was really beginning to see. The Father was revealing my negligence to me. I was getting to the bottom of what was going on inwardly. By repeatedly entrusting this place in me to others for safe keeping, I was leaving it open to being mistreated. It remained void of what could make it complete. This place was longing to be filled. It wanted to be fulfilled. Attention it craved. The longing inside needed to be satisfied. The emptiness there often to tears would me drive. This place served as the camping ground for my need to belong, be accepted, approved, and desired. My decisions and actions were stimulated by what was occupying this place. Every portion of my life is affected by what happens in this space.

This place, this space was my heart. That's where everything starts. Everything stems from what goes on in my heart. My lack of presence in this area of my life left me vulnerable to attacks. Sitting there I realized my heart had been under attack. *"Help me! My heart is under attack!"* I screamed desperately. *"Somebody please help me!"* I didn't begin to play the blame game. This was my fault because I wasn't on the job guarding my heart.

I sat in my car thinking out loud, *"This should not be surprising to me. I'm open for attacks. There is nothing I do to guard my heart regularly. I respond when something happens. The blame is on me for not paying attention. I should have protected me. Guarding my heart has not been on the top of my list. Actually, I rarely think about it. I'm managing so many other priorities that it feels self-centered to focus on me."*

Right there the Spirit revealed to me how I had been

deceived. My focus was on caring for others and paying very little attention to me. How could I care properly for others, how could I help others if I didn't see that taking care of me first was priority? He then brought this scripture back to my memory, *" A second is equally important: 'Love your neighbor as yourself."* Matthew 22:39 NLT. This was revelatory! The Father was attacking the erroneous thinking that had crippled me. He was being real and it was helping me. This verse basically said that I am to love others like I love me. It gave me the permission to focus on me while convicting me for not focusing on me simultaneously. It humbled me, convicted me, and corrected me. Hearing it was like receiving a blow to my chest. *"I see, I see, I see!"* I cried out as I acknowledged what was being revealed to me.

My living had been carefree. There was very little focus on caring for me. For instance, if someone hurt me, I'd reply, *"It's okay. I'm fine. I just want to make sure you're okay."* This was my way of trying to pretend it never occurred and that it didn't bother me. Not only would I say this to others, but I would say it to me. This was my attempt at treating each situation resolved when nothing had been solved.

My mind began reflecting on the situation which had driven me to that parking lot. I'd given the best of what I had to offer; and, was told in a passing conversation that I was no longer needed because someone else had been secured to finish what I'd started. Internally I responded, *"What? Is this really happening? I gave the best of me and could have changed whatever you needed. You didn't even give me an opportunity. I didn't even know you were looking for a replacement. You never mentioned it to me, but you chose to tell me in passing that you'd replaced me. Really!"* Externally I responded with a forced smile, *"That's fine. It's okay."* and after a very brief conversation, I continued on my way.

My internal conversation resumed while I walked to my car. *"You're irreplaceable, just a filler, you're not the real deal, they were always looking for another to replace you."* Getting in my car, I began to scream,

"It's not okay! You hurt me! Why do you keep doing this to me? I trusted you! I gave the best I had to offer to you! It's not okay! I'm not okay. You really hurt me. Why didn't I tell them? Why don't I ever tell them?" This was yet another example of my pattern of self-neglect. It's another example of how I did not guard my heart. The choices I made had not been very smart. This further revealed that my perception of what my heart could and could not handle was exaggerated.

Wow! That's why this pain was so severe. Everything stems from here. I admitted through the tears that had begun falling again, *"I've always had trouble in this area of my life."* This part of me has always suffered due to no management, poor management, or mismanagement, and has always been under attack. The Spirit showed me that this was nothing new. *"This has always been in operation in you."* Another snippet began to play in my head. This was a scene from my childhood. Yep! Back to my childhood we go. I believe He took me back because I needed to see how long I had been suffering these heart attacks. He wanted to show me my history.

The particular scene now playing out in my mind was of an incident that occurred when I was eleven years old. It was a Saturday Morning and my mom, brother, and I were preparing to spend the day shopping with cousins. Before leaving, I went to the kitchen to grab a quick bite to eat. When I opened the refrigerator door, I dropped an egg on the kitchen floor. Instead of cleaning up my mess, I left it there. When my mom entered the kitchen she asked, *"Who dropped this egg on the floor?"* Immediately I responded, *"Not me."* I lied naturally. My brother responded, *"Not me."* My mom then responded, *"Someone dropped this egg on the floor and until someone admits it we're not going anywhere."* My brother and I were in the room going back and forth refusing to accept the blame. Not wanting to admit I did it and ready to begin the day with our cousins, I told my brother, *"If you don't tell mommy you did it, we won't be able to go."* My brother went into the kitchen with tears falling from his eyes and said, *"Mommy, Tammy told me to tell you that I dropped the egg on the floor, but I didn't do it."*

Not only had I lied, but I deceived my brother into taking the blame. In my effort to escape the consequences of lying, I was willing to watch my brother pay the cost for my actions. All of this was done in an effort to avoid the disapproval of my mom. I didn't want to let her down. I thought her opinion of me might change, and she would love me less. You see, I've always longed for approval. To me approval = acceptance and acceptance = love.

Disapproval was like a stake being driven through my heart. Its wounds ran deep and would leave me filled with shame. Validation was critical for me. At the age of eleven, I didn't know about caring for that place deep within. I had no idea that disapproval of an action did not mean that you disapproved of me and that you could disapprove of my actions and still love me. I didn't know how to manage the place within me that determines what I do, and how I respond. I didn't know I needed to protect my heart.

Sitting in my car, the Spirit was revealing so much about me to me. My understanding of what was happening in me was increasing. My heart had been under attack. *"Why didn't anyone tell me how important it was to guard my heart? Did they tell me, but I chose to disregard? My challenges were all stemming from my lack of care. I know the attacks would still occur, but if I had measures in place these attacks would have never reached this space", I said internally.*

The Father was not done with me. There was more I needed to see. Because my heart remained unattended, the desire for acceptance, approval, and belonging continued to grow. What wasn't corrected in my childhood had now matured. It didn't disappear. The driving force behind whatever I did remained acceptance, approval, and a desire to belong. My chosen method for dealing with this perceived vacancy and anything that would attack this space was still lying with the intent to manipulate and deceive others into accepting, approving of, and receiving me. Just as I had done to others, someone was now doing to me.

This place in me, my heart, needed guarding, watching, and protecting. It needed a babysitter, and it was time to stop looking for others to fill the position. I didn't need a Nanny. This was my responsibility and because I wasn't present and on duty, my heart was constantly under attack. These attacks could have been avoided had I been on guard doing my part babysitting my heart.

෴5෴

DADDY, CAN I COME HOME?

All I wanted was to be accepted for me, but how could others accept who they didn't know nor could they see. Not only did I deceive others, I had deceived me. In my pursuit of acceptance, approval, and belonging, I submitted to much abuse, and misuse trying to be everything to everyone. The person I thought was me was one of the versions that had emerged to persuade others to accept me. What happened to me? What changed me? When did I abandon me? Did I ever really know me? I realize there were many images of me on the outside reflecting the many versions of me living inside. The real me was hiding beneath the versions created to protect me. When did this happen? When did I do this? How did I abandon me? ? I did this. I neglected me. It was me. I neglected me. I know this sounds crazy, maybe even bi-polar, or schizophrenic, but I had abandoned myself.

The habits I had assumed were not my own. They were things I had picked up attempting to become what others desired. Core to me and my personality was the desire to be accepted, approved, and to belong. There is nothing worse than not knowing where you fit, if you fit and if anyone cares. Uncertainty leaves you wondering why bother? Why try? You resolve within that your attempts, whatever they might be, won't make a difference anyway. You begin existing in oblivion as the world goes on around you with no one noticing that you have detached, vacated the premises, and are no longer there. No one asks or puts things on pause to check on you. In their minds, there is no reason to because they haven't noticed the changes that have taken place in you. Everything just keeps going communicating to you there is no need for you.

As I embraced this existence, I also began to internalize what I perceived as an unspoken message that came across loud and clear. Although it wasn't spoken the actions of others were communicating clearly. The message was painful, but I was convinced that I must accept it. I began to interpret through others actions and their lack of action that they wanted me to know, *"We can live with or without you! You are not a necessity. There are others who can do what you do for me. There is nothing unique or different about you. I can easily replace you. We were just settling for you, the imitation, awaiting the arrival of the real deal."*

What was wrong with me? Here I go again. Will this ever end? My heart was hurting. Sitting in that parking lot crying again I was trying to understand. *"Why do I keep doing this to myself? Why do I keep putting myself back in their hands?"* I asked myself as I began reminiscing again on the scene replaying in my mind which had driven me to my current state of hysteria.

I began to talk my way through each scene as if they

could hear me. *"I remember when you first approached me because you found something attractive about me. Something desirable. Something you could use. Yes, there was something in me that you thought would benefit you. It caught your eye. You pursued me. I didn't ask, but you offered. Yes, it was a good offer, but I was not the initiator. You saw something in me that you felt would help meet a need. I said yes because I knew I could fill the need. How could I stand by and watch you suffer knowing that I could help you? My love for you would not allow me to stand by and watch you suffer. What I did was out of love. No ulterior motives. Just love. Did I do something wrong? Should I have said no? Should ..."*

HELP ME LORD!!!!!!!!

"Father, you taught me better. I really don't have to live this way. I know better! Somewhere my eyes were diverted from you. Another caught my gaze. I don't know when or how, but shortly thereafter followed my heart. I acknowledge I was a willing participant. No one forced me. This isn't justifying whatever wrong others

have done, but I'm admitting where I went wrong. I bear
some responsibility. Continuing in self-deception, nor
self-manipulation will be added to my shame. Nope, I'm
not playing that game. I will not play the victim, nor act
like I was innocent prey. I played a role in what
happened to me. By no means am I blame free. I take
responsibility.

You have taught me better. Your instructions to me were
to KEEP, PROTECT, and GUARD my heart. You said to
watch and remain on alert at all times with the
awareness that I have an enemy just waiting for an
opportunity to hurt me, to destroy me. As you said it, I
could hear be intentional. Not haphazard, but
intentional. Forgive me, Father. I didn't obey. There's
no reason I should have surrendered myself as live prey.
I knew the enemy was lurking, looking, and waiting for
me. By whatever means, he wanted to cripple me. His
desire has always been to discredit me. He was after my
testimony because so many will overcome by the blood of
the Lamb, and the word of my testimony. I now know
and I knew then, but I still let him back in. When? I just

don't know when. I TAKE COMPLETE
RESPONSIBILITY FOR THE CONDITION OF MY
HEART.

The damage that has been done I allowed. I can't even
blame the enemy. The attacks and assault on my heart
were the result of my negligence or as my husband said
recently to me, "It's because you're optimistically
blind." I can't claim naivety. To say I was naïve
suggests I had a lack of information and was not familiar
with the tactics of the enemy. It wasn't that I didn't
know. I KNEW, but I did not APPLY what I KNEW.
Oh God! Help me! How do I get out of this? Is there a
way out? Did I go too far? I know I ignored you. I
disobeyed you. I did it repeatedly. How do I get out of
this? I feel so trapped. I'm so lost. I want out God! I
want out!

HELP ME, LORD!!!

When did I stop listening to you? How did I move so far
from you? Jesus, I didn't realize I'd left my safe place.
You're my safe place. When did I walk away from you?

Why didn't I recognize I'd walk away from you? We were so close. How could we be so close and I not realize I had moved so far from you? Can I come back in? Please, Father, let me back in. This doesn't feel right. Being separated from you doesn't feel good. I feel like raw meat left on the street for any hungry creature to consume. I feel so unprotected and vulnerable. It's not safe out here. Please let me come back to the safe place. I need to be covered. I want to be covered. Shield me, Lord. Hide me, please. I need your security.

PLEASE LORD, HELP ME!!!

I should not have listened to what I heard. I got caught up. Really, I thought I was missing something. Many said it did not take all of the sacrifice and that I was doing too much. I admit it got to me and I wanted to see if I could indulge and have you as well. Indulge and keep intimacy with you. I wanted both, your power and the pleasure. Yes, I know your Word says to choose one or the other, but it just seemed like I had already given up so much. What more could it cost?

Comfort became appealing. I started focusing on fitting in again. Reflecting, I just don't know when it happened. That enemy, he hooked me and then he hurt me. It's cold out here. My heart is broken. I can't blame anyone, but me. I left me open for attack. Deliver me. Father, please deliver me from me. I'm ready to return to you. I want to come home. All I want is to get back to my place of security.

Daddy, I'm not going to make it out here. Can I please come home?"

Heart's Cry

Oh God come in,

My heart can no longer take this pain,

Lord, please mend these broken pieces,

The recurring pain.

God, I'm ready for my heart to be whole again,

Right now God,

I'm ready to be like new again.

I've given out my heart when you told me you'd keep me.

I tried to fix it myself even when you said trust me.

Now my heart is bleeding,

Because of the pain that I welcomed in,

So here are my broken heart pieces,

Oh Lord please mend.

God, I'm ready for my heart to be whole again,

Right now God,

I'm ready to be like new again.

For you've taken my shattered pieces,

And you put them back together.

Now I know your love and it's ever so pure.

My heart is now in your hands,

And now I'm ready to love again.

Thank God I was ready and now my heart is whole again,

Right now I'm sure my heart is made whole again,

The pain from the past won't affect my heart's future,

Because God, You, have made my heart whole again,

Alyse A. Pope

MEET COACH TAMARA D. POPE

Coach Tamara's life mission is leading those she touches to liberty through Christ Jesus. Expressions of her mission are experienced through her family life, ministry, coaching, and writing. Next to her salvation, Tamara's greatest joy is being the wife of David M. Pope, and mother of Dante', Aurielle, and Alyse.

Daily, she aims to make every opportunity count realizing, "We must quickly carry out the tasks assigned us by the one who sent us.[a] The night is coming, and then no one can work." John 9:4 NLT.

Her heart's desire is to be pleasing in the Master's Eyes.

Additional Books By Author

My Time to Deal With It! Overcoming Strongholds

My Time to Let It Go! The Release

My Father Taught Me to FLI

You're Going to Make It Through
31 Days to Empower You

Keep Believing, You're Going to Break Through
31 Days to Empower You

Stepping Back to Strategize
Phase One: Something's Wrong in Me

Stepping Back to Strategize
Phase Two: Checking My Priorities

Contact Information

Website: www.thewritersnest.org

Email: tamaradpope@thewritersnest.org

www.ingramcontent.com/pod-product-compliance
Lightning Source LLC
Chambersburg PA
CBHW060200070426

42447CB00033B/2239